LIFE WITH ADHD

BY JAMES BOW

Published by The Child's World®
1980 Lookout Drive • Mankato, MN 56003-1705
800-599-READ • www.childsworld.com

Content Consultant: Jennifer G. Christner, M.D., Dean, School of Medicine, Baylor
College of Medicine

Photographs ©: Wave Break Media/Shutterstock Images, cover, 1; Oleksandr
Yuhlchek/Shutterstock Images, 5; iStockphoto, 6, 10; Shutterstock Images, 8, 13; Red
Tiger/Shutterstock Images, 14; Leonard Zhukovsky/Shutterstock Images, 16; Brian A.
Jackson/Shutterstock Images, 18

ISBN 9781503825055
LCCN 2017959676

Printed in the United States of America
PA02375

TABLE OF
CONTENTS

FAST FACTS

- ADHD stands for attention-deficit/**hyperactivity** disorder. People with ADHD have trouble focusing on things. They can't sit still, and they may sometimes act out suddenly, even **aggressively**.

- Kids with ADHD are often seen as "needing discipline," but the real issue is in the brain. The part of the brain that helps with learning, memory, and controlling emotions has developed differently than in other brains.

- According to the Centers for Disease Control and Prevention, approximately 6.4 million American children between the ages of four and 17 have ADHD. Adults can have ADHD as well, and many have had it since they were children.

- It is not known what causes ADHD. Scientists are still researching genes that may be involved.

- There is no cure for ADHD, but there are treatments. Certain medicines can help, with a doctor's **prescription**. Parents, teachers, and **counselors** can teach a child who has ADHD tools to manage their **symptoms**.

ADHD IN BOYS AND GIRLS

Boys are more likely to be **diagnosed** with ADHD than girls. As of 2012, these are the percentages of boys and girls who are diagnosed with ADHD in the United States.

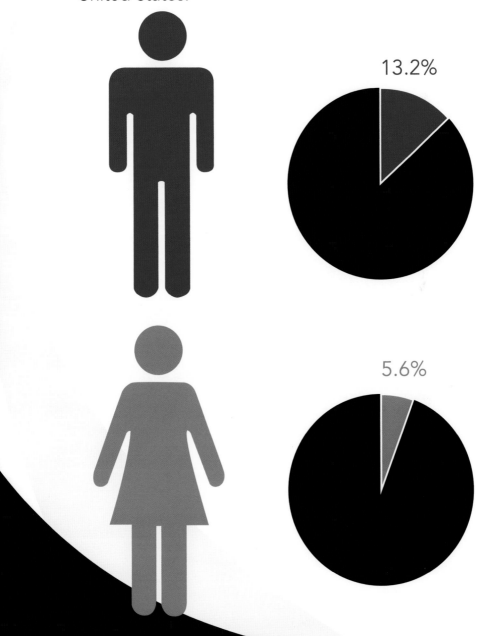

13.2%

5.6%

Chapter 1

UNABLE TO FOCUS

Becca snapped to attention. The teacher had called on her. But Becca didn't know what her teacher had said. The last thing she remembered was opening a textbook on math. Quickly, Becca looked down and read the answer to the last question.

The teacher shook her head no. The class had already moved on to spelling. Some of her fourth-grade classmates chuckled. Becca fidgeted, her cheeks flushing red.

It was the same every day. Becca tried to pay attention, but everything around her was so loud. Once, she found herself following the teacher's marker across the whiteboard, not seeing what the teacher was writing.

◄ ADHD can affect a child's memory and the ability to learn from mistakes.

▲ Talking to a teacher or therapist can help kids manage their ADHD.

Homework took so long she never had time to finish it. She had forgotten to bring it to school again today.

She wondered why she couldn't pay attention, no matter how hard she tried. Her family called her a daydreamer. It was too easy for Becca to get distracted.

Becca's mind whirled with all these thoughts so much, she missed her teacher calling on her again. She jerked up, her heart pounding.

To Becca's relief, the teacher told her that the counselor, Mr. Johnson, wanted to see her. Getting up, she wondered what he wanted, and if it had anything to do with the tests they made her take. Becca had taken several trips to the doctor where she was asked a lot of questions and had a physical exam.

ADHD FACTS

Boys with ADHD may often act out, run around, and hit things. Girls may withdraw and get anxious. Both boys and girls who have ADHD have difficulty focusing, which makes it harder for them to learn at school.

At Mr. Johnson's office, Becca's mother was there. Mr. Johnson told Becca that she had been diagnosed with ADHD. Mr. Johnson told her that it is nothing to be ashamed of. He told her that with patience and medicine, Becca would learn to manage her condition. This would help her improve at school.

Chapter 2

COOLING DOWN

Brett slammed the door of his room, and wished he could do it again.

His fists clenched as he remembered. There had been a substitute teacher at school today. Brett's classroom was too loud to learn anything. Then, when he came home, a neighbor waved to him. He told Brett to keep his cool and not kick down the door of his house. It was meant as a joke, but it hurt Brett's feelings. Brett had once gotten so mad he'd kicked in his front door.

Before Brett's parents took him to a **psychiatrist** and learned about his ADHD, the anger and stress in Brett's life would lead to meltdowns. Brett flinched with shame. He knew the neighbors talked about his past behavior.

◀ **It can be hard for people with ADHD to control their emotions.**

DIAGNOSING ADHD

There are different types of ADHD. The inattentive type is when a person has trouble focusing. A person with the hyperactive type feels full of energy and has trouble sitting still. Some have a combination of both types. Doctors diagnose ADHD if these symptoms are bad enough to affect a child's day-to-day life. The child will need to have a physical exam to rule out other problems. However, most children with ADHD do not get diagnosed at their first visit with the doctor. Usually, there are forms that parents and teachers need to fill out.

But Brett unclenched his fists, sat down, and pulled out his mood journal. Flipping open the page for today, he drew an angry face on the top line. Then he wrote down his thoughts. He wrote how he had been frustrated and angry after class because people had kept talking and he hadn't been able to understand the lessons.

Putting the pencil down, Brett felt calmer. He looked back at the days before. He'd had a meltdown on Tuesday.

▲ **Writing can help both kids and adults who have ADHD understand their feelings better and reduce stress.**

He had forgotten his medicine on Wednesday. Thursday was good, and his mother had given him a star sticker. Today, if there was no meltdown, Brett would receive another star.

Brett's journal entries were an outlet for his feelings and **impulses**. The stars were a nice way for his parents to show him that he was getting better.

Setting his journal aside, Brett got up and opened the door to his bedroom. He called down to his mother to come up, so he could talk to her about his day.

Chapter 3

ADHD GOLD

Michael had swum a great race, but he'd finished second. Standing on the podium beside the winner, he could feel the anger building inside him.

But then he saw his mother in the crowd. She smiled and held up her hand, cupping her fingers to make a letter "C." It was her signal to Michael to compose himself.

Michael was nine when he was diagnosed with ADHD. He had trouble in school. He couldn't sit still in class, and he often took things from his classmates. He hated reading and complained loudly about it.

His teachers didn't know what to do. So Michael's mother helped him. She gave him extra lessons at home.

◀ **Some scientists believe people with ADHD do better in individual sports like swimming than in group sports.**

▲ **Michael Phelps's teachers thought he might not ever be able to focus. Today, he has 28 Olympic medals.**

She also taught him ways to control his impulses, such as staying still until he was calm enough to let his energy out.

Michael's mother helped him channel his energy into swimming. He may have finished second in this race, but there would be others.

Michael later joined the United States Olympic team at the age of 15. He won his first Olympic gold medal when he was 19 and won 22 more gold medals after that.

Today, Michael Phelps has retired from swimming. He now runs the Michael Phelps Foundation. The organization helps children lead healthy and active lives. It provides swimming lessons to children around the world.

FAMOUS PEOPLE WITH ADHD

Actor Will Smith also had trouble paying attention in school. He feels he would have been diagnosed with ADHD had people known more about it at the time. American gymnast Simone Biles, like Michael Phelps, worked through her ADHD to become an Olympic gold medalist. Actor Channing Tatum also continues to work through his ADHD while starring in many movies.

Chapter 4

HANDLING THE UNEXPECTED

Jason stepped off the bus and breathed a sigh of relief. The buses had been on time. He walked happily to the gate where he would meet his friends to see the baseball game.

The world had been confusing and frustrating for Jason before his ADHD diagnosis five years ago. Then, Jason's counselor got together with him, his parents, and his fourth grade teachers and came up with a system.

One part of the system was to plan out his day. Jason knew when to do his chores and his homework. He broke his tasks into smaller pieces that he could handle. Then the world didn't seem so overwhelming anymore.

◄ Kids and adults with ADHD often have other mental health conditions as well, such as sleep disorders or depression.

But most of all, Jason had to figure out how to cope when something unexpected happened. When a plan fell apart, Jason felt like he was falling apart, too.

When Jason finally reached the gate, he saw that his friends weren't there. One part of the plan hadn't worked out. He breathed deeply and counted in his head until he calmed down. Then he pulled out his cell phone and texted his friend Brian.

Brian replied quickly. They were five minutes away, but they had the tickets. Jason could adjust his plan. He decided to go get snacks for himself and his friends while waiting.

MANAGING ADHD

Doctors say that having a schedule of chores and activities helps kids with ADHD deal with their day. Clear and simple rules help, along with rewards. Parents and kids need to work together and agree on what the rules and rewards are. With patience and attention, people can manage their ADHD and lead happy lives.

It still made Jason anxious when things didn't work according to plan, but he also knew he could adjust. It was hard work, but knowing he could handle it made him feel good.

As Jason came back with the snacks, he saw the bus pull up and his friends step off. They waved and came over. Jason managed to work through the unexpected, one step at a time.

THINK ABOUT IT

- Do you find it easy or more difficult to concentrate when people around you are noisy? How do you focus?
- What do you do to calm yourself down? Do you write in a journal or listen to music, or is there another activity that works for you?
- Have you ever made a plan and then had something happen that interrupted it? How did you handle it?
- How could you be good to a friend who has ADHD?

GLOSSARY

aggressively (uh-GRES-iv-lee): To act aggressively is to behave angrily, forcefully, or violently. Sometimes kids with ADHD will act aggressively toward their parents.

counselors (KOUN-suh-lerz): Counselors are people trained to give advice about problems. Counselors helped Jake's parents and teachers come up with a plan to handle his ADHD.

diagnosed (dye-uhg-NOHSSED): To be diagnosed means to identify what is wrong with someone or something by checking the signs of a problem. The doctor ran tests on Brett and diagnosed Brett with ADHD.

hyperactivity (hye-pur-ak-TIV-ih-tee): Hyperactivity is the state of being much more active than normal. Brett struggled with his hyperactivity when he was unable to keep still and quiet.

impulses (IM-puhlss-ez): Impulses are sudden actions that often happen without thinking about it. Michael didn't always know how to control his impulses.

prescription (preh-SKRIP-shuhn): A prescription is a note a doctor writes out that allows someone to get and take a certain medicine. Becca got a prescription for medicine to help her feel less stressed.

psychiatrist (sye-KYE-uh-trist): A psychiatrist is a doctor who works with mental health issues. The psychiatrist listened to Brett's problems and set up a treatment plan that could help.

symptoms (SIMP-tuhms): Symptoms are things that suggest a person has a medical problem. Becca's difficulty staying focused was one of the symptoms of her ADHD.

TO LEARN MORE

Books

Kraus, Jeanne. *Get Ready for Jetty! My Journal about ADHD and Me.* Washington, DC: Magination Press, 2013.

Quinn, Patricia O. *Attention, Girls! A Guide to Learn All about Your AD/HD.* Washington, DC: Magination Press, 2009.

Stumpf, Tobias. *Journal of an ADHD Kid: The Good, the Bad, and the Useful.* Bethesda, MD: Woodbine House, 2014.

Web Sites

Visit our Web site for links about ADHD:

childsworld.com/links

Note to Parents, Teachers, and Librarians: We routinely verify our Web links to make sure they are safe and active sites. So encourage your readers to check them out!

SELECTED BIBLIOGRAPHY

Gregoire, Carolyn. "People with ADHD Have Different Brains." *Huffington Post.* Oath, Inc., 24 Feb. 2017. Web. 25 Jan. 2018.

Hallowell, Edward M., and John J. Ratey. *Driven to Distraction: Recognizing and Coping with Attention Deficit Disorder from Childhood through Adulthood.* New York, NY: Simon & Schuster, 2011. Print.

McGlensey, Melissa, "18 People Explain What ADHD Feels Like." *The Mighty.* Mighty Proud Media, Inc., 26 Feb. 2016. Web. 25 Jan. 2018.

INDEX

ABOUT THE AUTHOR

James Bow is the author of more than 40 nonfiction books for children. He is a graduate of the University of Waterloo in Ontario, Canada, and a freelance writer and editor. He currently lives outside Toronto, Canada, with his wife and two daughters.

24